Praying
the
Rosary

Missionary Oblates of Mary Immaculate
National Shrine of Our Lady of the Snows
Belleville IL 62223-4694

Library of Congress Cataloging-in-Publication Data
Praying the rosary.—1st large print ed
    p.   cm.
   ISBN 0-8027-2671-2
   1. Rosary. I. Walker and Company.
[BX2163.P73   1992]
242'.74—dc20   92-410
                 CIP

Printed in the United States of America.

Published by Walker and Company
for Missionary Oblates of Mary Immaculate

Contents

Praying the
Rosary

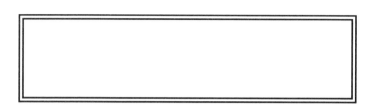

History of the Rosary

The Rosary, after the Mass, is the most popular of Catholic devotions. It has brought, and continues to bring, great comfort to Catholics the world over for centuries. It is said on a string of beads, which can be anything from crystal to silver or gold or plain wood.

This string consists of five groups of beads called decades. Each group has eleven beads: ten small beads and one large bead. The group begins with the "Our Father" said on the large bead. The "Hail Mary" is then said on each of the ten small beads. And, at the end of each decade is said the "Glory Be."

The complete Rosary consists of fifteen decades (a total of 165 beads). In turn, the decades are divided into three groups of five, which are called the Mysteries of the lives of Our Lord Jesus Christ and his Blessed Virgin Mother Mary.

While praying the first group of five, one should meditate on the Joyful Mysteries, which are usually said on Mondays and Thursdays (see page 21).

While praying the second group of five, one should meditate on the Sorrowful Mysteries, which are usually said on Tuesdays and Fridays (see page 53).

And while praying the third group of five, one meditates on the Glorious Mysteries, which are usually said on Wednesdays, Saturdays, and Sundays (see page 83).

To say the full Rosary is to meditate and pray on all fifteen Mysteries. However, in practicality, when one speaks of "praying the Rosary," it is usually meant once around the beads, or five decades, meditating on one set of Mysteries at a time.

Legend has it that the Blessed Virgin Mary appeared to St. Dominic (d. 1221), founder of the Order of Friars Preachers, and presented him with the Rosary during his work to convert the Albigensian heretics of France back to the true faith. As wonderful as this story is, it is just a story, having been first introduced into a late–fourteenth-century life of St. Dominic. However, the presence of this legend does show that the Rosary has been a centerpiece of Dominican devotion for a long time and that the friars preached it enthusiastically to the people they taught.

As with practically everything, the Rosary as we know it today is a product of gradual development. St. Benedict of Nursia, in Italy, a hermit of the sixth century, exhorted his disciples to pray the 150 psalms of the ancient psalter at least once a week. Since the monasteries were frequently in the middle of the town they served and the townspeople gathered in the monastery church to worship, it was natural that the prayers of the laity would be inspired by the monks praying the psalms. But the psalms were too complicated and long for the uneducated laity.

In order to help the laity join in the prayers, the psalms developed into the saying of 150 "Our Fathers" with a string of beads to keep count.

In addition to the full psalter prayed by the monks, they also celebrated a "little office" of the Blessed Virgin Mary every day alongside the "Our Fathers" of the laity. As time went by, the prayer to Mary, based on the words from Luke's Gospel

(Luke 1:28, 42), replaced the "Our Fathers," again perhaps because the shorter lines of the "Hail Mary" were easier to remember and say than the longer prayer to the Father. Over the centuries, the various lines of the "Hail Mary" were added until, in the sixteenth century, the prayer as we know it today was said. At the same time, the "Glory Be" was being added to the end of each decade.

The beads themselves were evolving from a continuous string of 150 to one of fifty, which was used three times a day. Eventually, by the thirteenth century, the fifty beads were divided into five groups of ten small beads for the "Hail Marys" and one large bead for the "Our Father."

In the thirteenth century, Thomas of Contimpre called this string of beads a *rosarium,* a rose garden, from which our word *rosary* developed. The symbolic white roses for joy, red roses for sorrow, and yellow roses for glory, together with thorns, have taken their place as important metaphors for the pray-er of the Rosary.

The fifteen Mysteries of the Rosary, as well, developed over the centuries. When the psalter was sung by the monks and nuns, they added certain reflections, frequently drawn from Scripture, to fit a particular feast or season. This, too, was carried over to the prayers of the laity. St. Bernard of Clairvaux (d. 1153) is considered to be the author of one of the earliest collections of spiritual reflections on the joys that Mary experienced throughout her life. In the fifteen century, Henry Egher of Kolkar, a Carthusian monk, was the first to clearly set forth a Rosary of fifteen decades, and the scriptural reflections also came to be reduced to fifteen. By the end of the fifteenth century, the Mysteries that we know today were used throughout the Church.

The Rosary has been a special prayer of the popes of the Catholic Church. A declaration of Pope Sixtus IV in 1479 was the first to extol the Rosary. In the sixteenth century, Pope Saint Pius V established October 7 as the Feast of the Most Holy Rosary. During the apparitions of Mary to Bernadette at Lourdes in 1858, the Blessed Virgin was seen with a long Rosary over her arm. At Fatima in 1917, Mary herself taught one of the visionaries, Jacinta, how to pray the Rosary and during the last apparition, just before the miracle of the dancing sun, Mary called herself the Lady of the Rosary. Pope John Paul II has a special devotion to Mary through the Rosary and has written often on the need to pray the Rosary.

But, most important, the Rosary is meaningful because Catholics love it and truly enjoy saying it. Popes and saints may encourage the saying of the Rosary in official pronouncements, but they are just reiterating what the laity have already taken to heart. The Rosary began to help the laity join in the complicated prayers of the monks and nuns and it remains today the people's prayer. It helps us retreat from the chaos of our daily lives into a simpler time and allows us for a while to slow down and meditate. It refreshes us, comforts us, and connects us to life's deepest mysteries.

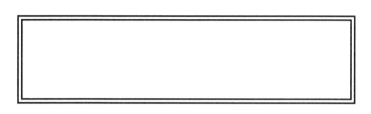

INTRODUCTION TO
THE REFLECTIONS

By Father Ron Lengwin,
director of public affairs,
Catholic Diocese of
Pittsburgh

The Rosary may be likened to a
chain of unbreakable love. When we
pray it, our entire being is invited to
participate—body, mind, and spirit;
heart and soul—so that we can place
ourselves in the presence of God,
and deepen our love for Jesus and
Mary, his mother. As we prayerfully

reflect on how God's love enlight-
ened, strengthened, and guided
them in the life they shared, we discover that this same love is available
to us in every moment of life. We
look back at their lives to better understand how God interacts in our
lives today. And those events that at
first appear to be mysteries soon become clear revelations of God's love
for us, and sources of joy no one can
take away from us.

Although we may choose at
times to concentrate on the beads
and the words of the prayers themselves, it is not the best way to
pray the Rosary. Our focus must be
on the meaning of the Mysteries
we are reflecting on. For this form
of prayer invites us to withdraw to
that part of our being that belongs
to God alone—to enter into an inti-
mate relationship with God. It
should not surprise us then that

Pope John Paul has said the Rosary is his favorite prayer.

When you pray the Rosary, discover how important you are to God by reflecting on the many ways God has entered your life.

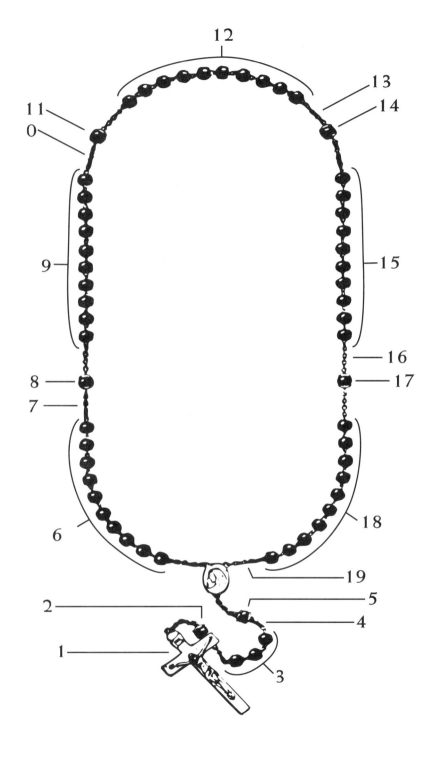

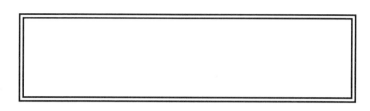

HOW TO PRAY
THE ROSARY

(See number references on opposite page.)

1. Make the Sign of the Cross and say the Apostles' Creed.
2. Say the Our Father.
3. Say three Hail Marys.
4. Say the Glory Be to the Father.
5. Say the first Mystery; then the Our Father.
6. Say ten Hail Marys.
7. Say the Glory Be to the Father.

8. Say the second Mystery; then the Our Father.
9. Say ten Hail Marys.
10. Say the Glory Be to the Father.
11. Say the third Mystery; then the Our Father.
12. Say ten Hail Marys.
13. Say the Glory Be to the Father.
14. Say the fourth Mystery; then the Our Father.
15. Say ten Hail Marys.
16. Say the Glory Be to the Father.
17. Say the fifth Mystery; then the Our Father.
18. Say ten Hail Marys.
19. Say the Glory Be to the Father.

Say the Prayer after the Rosary (see page 18).

The Prayers of the Rosary

☐ THE SIGN OF THE CROSS
In the name of the Father
  and of the Son,
    and of the Holy Spirit. Amen.

☐ THE APOSTLES' CREED
I believe in God,
  the Father Almighty,
  Creator of heaven and earth.
And in Jesus Christ,
  his only Son, our Lord,
  who was conceived by the Holy
    Spirit,
  born of the Virgin Mary,

suffered under Pontius Pilate,
>   was crucified,
>   died,
>   and was buried.
He descended into hell.
The third day he rose from the dead.
He ascended into heaven
>   and sits at the right hand of God,
>   the Father Almighty.
From thence he shall come to judge
>   the living and the dead.
I believe in the Holy Spirit,
>   the Holy Catholic Church,
>   the communion of saints,
>   the forgiveness of sins,
>   the resurrection of the body,
>   and life everlasting. Amen.

☐ THE OUR FATHER
Our Father, who art in heaven,
Hallowed be thy name.
Thy kingdom come,
Thy will be done,
On earth
>   as it is in heaven.

Give us this day our daily bread;
And forgive us our trespasses
As we forgive those who trespass
against us;
And lead us not into temptation,
but deliver us from evil.
Amen.

☐ THE HAIL MARY
Hail Mary, full of grace!
The Lord is with thee!
Blessed art thou among women,
and blessed is the fruit of thy womb
Jesus.
Holy Mary, Mother of God,
pray for us sinners now,
and at the hour of our death. Amen.

☐ THE GLORY BE
Glory be to the Father,
and to the Son,
and to the Holy Spirit.
As it was in the beginning,
is now, and ever will be,
world without end. Amen.

☐ A PRAYER AFTER THE ROSARY

O God, whose only-begotten Son, by his life, death, and Resurrection, has opened to us the rewards of eternal life, grant, we beseech you, that meditating on these mysteries of the holy Rosary of the Blessed Virgin Mary, we may imitate what they contain and obtain what they promise. Through our Lord and Savior Jesus Christ. Amen.

The Joyful
Mysteries

The First Joyful Mystery

☐ The Annunciation

In the sixth month, the angel Gabriel was sent from God to a town of Galilee called Nazareth, to a virgin betrothed to a man named Joseph, of the house of David, and the virgin's name was Mary.

And coming to her, he said, "Hail, favored one! The Lord is with you." But she was greatly troubled at what was said and pondered what sort of greeting this might be. Then the angel said to her, "Do not be afraid, Mary, for you have found favor with God. Behold, you will conceive in your womb and bear a son, and you shall name him Jesus. He will be great and will be called Son of the Most High, and the Lord God will give him the throne of David his father, and he will rule over the house of Jacob forever, and of his kingdom there will be no end." But Mary said to the angel, "How can this be, since I have no relations with a man?" And the angel said to her in reply, "The holy Spirit will come upon you, and the power of the Most High will overshadow you. Therefore the child to be born will be called holy, the Son of God. And behold, Elizabeth, your relative, has also conceived a son in her old age, and this is the sixth month for her who was called barren; for nothing will be impossible for God." Mary said, "Behold, I am the handmaid of the Lord. May it be done to me according to your word." Then the angel departed from her.

Luke 1:26–38

REFLECTION ON THE FIRST JOYFUL MYSTERY

The First Joyful Mystery is the Annunciation. God comes to Mary in a special way in the archangel Gabriel who reveals that God has selected her to be the mother of his Son. As we reflect on this event, we can think of special moments in our own lives when God has come to us in family members, in friends, and even in complete strangers who have helped to bring out the best in us from those hidden sources of goodness and love invested in us by God.

We, like Mary, have stored many thoughts and impressions in the memory banks of our hearts, and perhaps a few questions only God can answer someday. Included are the names of people who have taught us how precious life is and how powerful love is. Our very being is composed of the love and the life they have shared with us. Did you ever wonder if God sent them to you and if there may have been an angel among them? Think about someone who has been special to you and send them some of your love as you pray. Ask an angel to take it to them. Include Mary among them.

SAY ONE *OUR FATHER;*
TEN *HAIL MARYS;*
ONE *GLORY BE TO THE FATHER.*

My Own Reflection on the First Joyful Mystery

The Second Joyful Mystery

☐ The Visitation

During those days Mary set out and traveled to the hill country in haste to a town of Judah, where she entered the house of Zechariah and greeted Elizabeth. When Elizabeth heard Mary's greeting, the infant leaped in her womb, and Elizabeth, filled with the holy Spirit, cried out in a loud voice and said, "Most blessed are you among women, and blessed is the fruit of your womb. And how does this happen to me, that the mother of my Lord should come to me? For at

the moment the sound of your greeting reached my ears, the infant in
my womb leaped for joy. Blessed are
you who believed that what was spo-
ken to you by the Lord would be fulfilled."
And Mary said:

"My soul proclaims the greatness
        of the Lord;
 my spirit rejoices in God my
        savior.
For he has looked upon his
        handmaid's lowliness;
 behold, from now on will all
        ages call me blessed.
The Mighty One has done great
        things for me,
 and holy is his name.
His mercy is from age to age
 to those who fear him.
He has shown might with his
        arm,
 dispersed the arrogant of mind
        and heart.

He has thrown down the rulers
    from their thrones
 but lifted up the lowly.
The hungry he has filled with
    good things;
 the rich he has sent away
    empty.
He has helped Israel his servant,
 remembering his mercy,
according to his promise to our
    fathers,
 to Abraham and to his descendants
    forever."

Mary remained with her about three
months and then returned to her
home.

Luke 1:39–56

REFLECTION ON THE SECOND JOYFUL MYSTERY

The Second Joyful Mystery is the Visitation. Mary makes a journey prompted by the love in her heart to visit her cousin, Elizabeth, who is pregnant with John the Baptist. Having learned the lesson that nothing is impossible with God, Mary and Elizabeth share the kind of joy that God must have felt after he created the world and made man in his own image and likeness. God participated in the birth of their sons as he did in our birth and does in the birth of every child.

We are reminded that the impossible can happen when we invite God to be a part of everything we say and do. We must freely open our hearts to receive God's love, for there is nothing in life that shuts tighter than a heart that rejects love. Even God's love will not enter where it is not welcome. Mary and Elizabeth said yes to God. Is there anything in your life that God has been waiting for you to say yes to?

SAY ONE *OUR FATHER;*
TEN *HAIL MARYS;*
ONE *GLORY BE TO THE FATHER.*

My Own Reflection on the Second Joyful Mystery

THE THIRD JOYFUL MYSTERY

☐ THE NATIVITY

In those days a decree went out from Caesar Augustus that the whole world should be enrolled. This was the first enrollment, when Quirinius was governor of Syria. So all went to be enrolled, each to his own town. And Joseph too went up from Galilee from the town of Nazareth to Judea, to the city of David that is called Bethlehem, because he was of the house and family of David, to be enrolled with Mary, his betrothed, who was with child. While they were there, the time came for her to have her child, and she gave birth to her firstborn son. She wrapped him in swaddling clothes and laid him in a manger, because there was no room for them in the inn.

Now there were shepherds in that region living in the fields and keeping the night watch over their flock. The angel of the Lord appeared to them and the glory of the Lord shone around them, and they were struck with great fear. The angel said to them, "Do not be afraid; for behold, I proclaim to you good news of great joy that will be for all the people. For today in the city of David a savior has been born for you who is Messiah and Lord. And this will be a sign for you: you will find an infant wrapped in swaddling clothes and lying in a manger." And suddenly there was a multitude of the heavenly host with the angel, praising God and saying:

"Glory to God in the highest
and on earth peace to those
on whom his favor rests."

When the angels went away
from them to heaven, the shepherds
said to one another, "Let us go,
then, to Bethlehem to see this thing
that has taken place, which the Lord
has made known to us." So they
went in haste and found Mary and
Joseph, and the infant lying in the
manger.

When they saw this, they made
known the message that had been
told them about this child. All who
heard it were amazed by what had
been told them by the shepherds.
And Mary kept all these things, reflecting on them in her heart. Then
the shepherds returned, glorifying
and praising God for all they had
heard and seen, just as it had been
told to them.

LUKE 2:1–20

REFLECTION ON THE
THIRD JOYFUL MYSTERY

The Third Joyful Mystery is the Nativity. Jesus, the Son of God, enters the world. God reaches out to us with love so that we may reach out to one another in the same way. For love that is not shared dies. There are many gifts that we can give to one another, but there is no better gift than a portion of ourself—of our life, of our love. In the giving of these gifts we bless each other. We give people new life by believing in them, by giving them hope, by showing them how lovable they are, by sharing their pain.

Open your heart now and ask God to fill it with the warmth of his love so that new life may be born in you.

SAY ONE *OUR FATHER;*
TEN *HAIL MARYS;*
ONE *GLORY BE TO THE FATHER.*

My Own Reflection on
the Third Joyful Mystery

The Fourth Joyful Mystery

☐ The Presentation of Jesus
   in the Temple

When the days were completed for
their purification according to the
law of Moses, they took him up to
Jerusalem to present him to the
Lord, just as it is written in the law
of the Lord, "Every male that opens
the womb shall be consecrated to
the Lord," and to offer the sacrifice
of "a pair of turtledoves or two
young pigeons," in accordance with
the dictate in the law of the Lord.

     Now there was a man in Jerusalem whose name was Simeon. This man was righteous and devout, awaiting the consolation of Israel, and the holy Spirit was upon him.

It had been revealed to him by the holy Spirit that he should not see death before he had seen the Messiah of the Lord. He came in the Spirit into the temple; and when the parents brought in the child Jesus to perform the custom of the law in regard to him, he took him into his arms and blessed God, saying:

"Now, Master, you may let your
     servant go
 in peace, according to your
     word,
for my eyes have seen your salvation,
 which you prepared in sight
     of all the peoples,
a light for revelation to the Gentiles,
 and glory for your people Israel."

The child's father and mother

were amazed at what was said about him; and Simeon blessed them and said to Mary his mother, "Behold, this child is destined for the fall and rise of many in Israel, and to be a sign that will be contradicted (and you yourself a sword will pierce) so that the thoughts of many hearts may be revealed." There was also a prophetess, Anna, the daughter of Phanuel, of the tribe of Asher. She was advanced in years, having lived seven years with her husband after her marriage, and then as a widow until she was eighty-four. She never left the temple, but worshiped night and day with fasting and prayer.

And coming forward at that very time, she gave thanks to God and spoke about the child to all who were awaiting the redemption of Jerusalem.

LUKE 2:22–38

REFLECTION ON THE FOURTH JOYFUL MYSTERY

The Fourth Joyful Mystery is the Presentation in the Temple. Mary and Jesus, accompanied by Joseph, go to the temple on the fortieth day after his birth to be sanctified according to Jewish law. They are met there by Simeon and Anna, who had lived long lives of constant prayer in preparation for this moment when they would see the face of God.

What hopes and dreams do you have? Do you live with a sense of expectation—wondering what God

will do for you next and eager to
know what you can do for God? He
wants us to prayerfully prepare ourselves to be sanctified by the power
of his love—to become all that he
created us to be and to use our gifts
as he intended. When was the last
time you did something for God
alone? Deepen your prayer life and
allow God to surprise you. Is there
any greater gift than the surprise of
love, especially when it comes from
God?

SAY ONE *OUR FATHER;*
TEN *HAIL MARYS;*
ONE *GLORY BE TO THE FATHER.*

My Own Reflection on
the Fourth Joyful Mystery

THE FIFTH JOYFUL MYSTERY

☐ THE FINDING OF JESUS IN
  THE TEMPLE

Each year his parents went to Jerusalem for the feast of Passover, and when he was twelve years old, they went up according to festival custom. After they had completed its days, as they were returning, the boy Jesus remained behind in Jerusalem, but his parents did not know it. Thinking that he was in the caravan, they journeyed for a day and looked for him among their relatives and acquaintances, but not finding him, they returned to Jerusalem to look for him. After three days they found him in the temple, sitting in the midst of the teachers, listening to them and asking them questions, and all who heard him were astounded at his understanding and his answers. When his parents saw him, they were astonished, and his mother said to him, "Son, why have you done this to us? Your father and I have been looking for you with great anxiety." And he said to them, "Why were you looking for me? Did you not know that I must be in my Father's house?" But they did not understand what he said to them. He went down with them and came to Nazareth, and was obedient to them; and his mother kept all these things in her heart.

And Jesus advanced [in] wisdom and age and favor before God and man.

Luke 2:41–52

REFLECTION ON THE FIFTH JOYFUL MYSTERY

The Fifth Joyful Mystery is the finding in the temple. When Joseph and Mary cannot find Jesus, they go looking for him and discover he has been in the temple, listening to the rabbis debate, perhaps even engaging in debate with them at the age of twelve. He explains he had to do his father's will. How obedient are we to the will of God?

We all know the joy of finding something that has been lost, or renewing a relationship that has been broken. Is there a relationship in your life that needs some attention from you—that needs to be healed? You have the power of God's love within you to effect such a cure. Prayer can help you to find that power.

May you feel the warmth of God's love in your life today, and may it be for you a gentle and joy-filled day.

SAY ONE *OUR FATHER;*
TEN *HAIL MARYS;*
ONE *GLORY BE TO THE FATHER.*

My Own Reflection on the Fifth Joyful Mystery

The
Sorrowful
Mysteries

The First Sorrowful Mystery

☐ Jesus' Agony in the Garden
Then they came to a place named Gethsemane, and he said to his disciples, "Sit here while I pray."

He took with him Peter, James, and John, and began to be troubled and distressed. Then he said to them, "My soul is sorrowful even to death. Remain here and keep watch." He advanced a little and fell to the ground and prayed that if it were possible the hour might pass by him; he said, "Abba, Father, all things are possible to you. Take this cup away from me, but not what I will but what you will."

When he returned he found them asleep. He said to Peter, "Simon, are you asleep? Could you not keep watch for one hour? Watch and pray that you may not undergo the test. The spirit is willing but the flesh is weak." Withdrawing again, he prayed, saying the same thing.

Then he returned once more and found them asleep, for they could not keep their eyes open and did not know what to answer him. He returned a third time and said to them, "Are you still sleeping and taking your rest? It is enough. The hour has come. Behold, the Son of Man is to be handed over to sinners. Get up, let us go. See, my betrayer is at hand."

MARK 14:32–42

REFLECTION ON THE
FIRST SORROWFUL MYSTERY

Jesus is under severe emotional strain in the Garden of Gethsemane. He walks alone while his disciples sleep. Every breath and every beat of his heart are prayers asking for courage and strength to endure the pain that awaits him. We, too, have been in that garden when we face a serious illness, the death of a loved one, or any of the myriad traumas that life can throw at us. And prayerfully from the depths of our being, we find the wisdom and the strength we need—gifts placed there by God.

    With eyes of faith, imagine Jesus collapsing to the ground; leaning on a rock, and praying, as we have at times for all we're worth: "My Father, if it is possible, let this suffering pass me by." When we find ourselves in Gethsemane, do we have enough faith to place ourselves entirely in God's care? Faith is more than positive thinking. Faith means that no matter what has happened in life, we still believe and trust in the powerful love of God. Nothing can separate us from God's love.

SAY ONE *OUR FATHER;*
TEN *HAIL MARYS;*
ONE *GLORY BE TO THE FATHER.*

My Own Reflection on
the First Sorrowful Mystery

The Second Sorrowful Mystery

☐ Jesus Is Scourged
So Pilate, wishing to satisfy the
crowd, released Barabbas to them
and, after he had Jesus scourged,
handed him over to be crucified.

Mark 15:15

REFLECTION ON THE
SECOND SORROWFUL MYSTERY

The soldiers bring Jesus to the court-
yard where he is to be scourged. We
have been beaten by life at times.
We have scars on our hearts to prove
it. But we have also whipped others
through our insensitivity, selfish-
ness, and thoughtlessness. If we
could see the harm our sins have
caused, would we despair or would
we change our ways?

No matter how much we
would like to minimize or deny evil,
it exists in the world. We do not

want to believe we work for the evil one when we sin. And we may not truly understand how powerful God's goodness is until we experience how terrifying evil is. We see the constant struggle between good and evil as the soldiers untie Jesus and prepare for him to be beaten with vicious lashes that will stagger him.

The pain from his scourging is so terrible that Jesus must fight for breath. Some of life's struggles must be fought alone. Or at least it seems that way until we discover that the mystery of God's love touches every moment of life, until we discover that our love can make the difference between failure or success in someone's life.

SAY ONE *OUR FATHER;*
TEN *HAIL MARYS;*
ONE *GLORY BE TO THE FATHER.*

My Own Reflection on the Second Sorrowful Mystery

THE THIRD SORROWFUL MYSTERY

☐ JESUS IS CROWNED WITH
   THORNS

The soldiers led him away inside
the palace, that is, the praetorium,
and assembled the whole cohort.
   They clothed him in purple
and, weaving a crown of thorns,
placed it on him. They began to sa-
lute him with, "Hail, King of the
Jews!" and kept striking his head
with a reed and spitting upon him.
They knelt before him in homage.
And when they had mocked him,
they stripped him of the purple

cloak, dressed him in his own clothes, and led him out to crucify him.

Mark 15:16–20

REFLECTION ON THE
THIRD SORROWFUL MYSTERY

Picture Jesus in terrible agony,
beaten and bleeding, crowned mock-
ingly with thorns. Many sights
move us to tears. Sometimes they
are necessary to water the seeds of
hope God has planted in our hearts.
Holy water has been described as
the tears of angels that remind us
God has not forgotten us and always
comes when we call upon his Son. A
saint is not a person who never fails,
but one who never quits when he or
she does fail.

Life occasionally seems too cruel to endure. The concept of a loving God seems foolish. We work hard and pray unceasingly but without any visible results. Explanations and words of encouragement seem empty. Why go on, we wonder. And then we discover we may have to die a little to make room for new life and greater love from God.

SAY ONE *OUR FATHER*;
TEN *HAIL MARYS*;
ONE *GLORY BE TO THE FATHER*.

My Own Reflection on
the Third Sorrowful Mystery

THE FOURTH SORROWFUL MYSTERY

☐ THE CARRYING OF THE CROSS
As they led him away they took hold
of a certain Simon, a Cyrenian, who
was coming in from the country;
and after laying the cross on him,
they made him carry it behind Jesus.
A large crowd of people followed
Jesus, including many women who
mourned and lamented him. Jesus·
turned to them and said, "Daugh-
ters of Jerusalem, do not weep for
me; weep instead for yourselves and
for your children, for indeed, the
days are coming when people will

say, 'Blessed are the barren, the wombs that never bore and the breasts that never nursed.' At that time people will say to the mountains, 'Fall upon us!' and to the hills, 'Cover us!' for if these things are done when the wood is green what will happen when it is dry?" Now two others, both criminals, were led away with him to be executed.

Luke 23:26–32

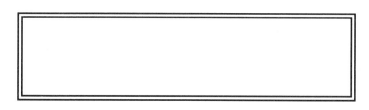

REFLECTION ON THE FOURTH SORROWFUL MYSTERY

Can you hear the cross scraping on the ground behind Jesus? Many people carry crosses today, not on their shoulders but in their hearts. They have such names as pain, sorrow, and loneliness.

On the road to Calvary, Jesus meets a group of women. As the shadow of the cross falls upon them, he tells them not to weep for him but to worry about themselves and all the struggles they will have to face in the future. In the midst of his pain as he carries the weight of every sin, Jesus still comforts others. A lighted candle, we are told, does not lose anything when it gives light to another candle, and neither does a heart that gives love to another heart.

Do you think Jesus wanted to see his mother on the way to his crucifixion? Or did he want to spare her that pain? But he knew her well enough to know she would be there. And she was. What do you see in his eyes and in her eyes when they meet?

SAY ONE *OUR FATHER;*
TEN *HAIL MARYS;*
ONE *GLORY BE TO THE FATHER.*

My Own Reflection on
the Fourth Sorrowful Mystery

THE FIFTH SORROWFUL MYSTERY

☐ THE CRUCIFIXION OF JESUS
They gave him wine drugged with
myrrh, but he did not take it. Then
they crucified him and divided his
garments by casting lots for them to
see what each should take. It was
nine o'clock in the morning when
they crucified him. The inscription
of the charge against him read, "The
King of the Jews." With him they
crucified two revolutionaries, one on
his right and one on his left. Those
passing by reviled him, shaking
their heads and saying, "Aha! You

who would destroy the temple and rebuild it in three days, save yourself by coming down from the cross." Likewise the chief priests, with the scribes, mocked him among themselves and said, "He saved others; he cannot save himself. Let the Messiah, the King of Israel, come down now from the cross that we may see and believe." Those who were crucified with him also kept abusing him.

At noon darkness came over the whole land until three in the afternoon. And at three o'clock Jesus cried out in a loud voice, *"Eloi, Eloi, lema sabachthani?"* which is translated, "My God, my God, why have you forsaken me?" Some of the bystanders who heard it said, "Look, he is calling Elijah." One of them ran, soaked a sponge with wine, put it on a reed, and gave it to him to drink, saying, "Wait, let us see if Elijah comes to take him down." Jesus gave a loud cry and breathed

his last. The veil of the sanctuary
was torn in two from top to bottom.
When the centurion who stood fac-
ing him saw how he breathed his
last he said, "Truly this man was
the Son of God!" There were also
women looking on from a distance.
Among them were Mary Magdalene,
Mary the mother of the younger
James and of Joses, and Salome.
These women had followed him
when he was in Galilee and minis-
tered to him. There were also many
other women who had come up with
him to Jerusalem.

Mark 15:23–41

REFLECTION ON THE
FIFTH SORROWFUL MYSTERY

Jesus hangs lifeless on the cross. The rain from the storm that erupted when he died washes the blood and sweat from his body before he is taken down and placed in the arms of Mary, his mother. Her tears anoint him. What do you feel when you see his bruised, broken body? Without love in our hearts, it is easy to conclude that the crucifixion of Christ is the sad story of a fool. If it isn't, why haven't our lives changed? Why do we allow habitual sins to control us and rule our lives? Hasn't Jesus done enough for us?

Love does not take away all sorrow and pain, but it does teach us that what is really important in life is not when you die or how you die, but how you have lived and loved. Place your sins at the foot of the cross, and receive love from Christ that will renew you. The crucifix reminds us how precious life is and how powerful love is.

SAY ONE *OUR FATHER;*
TEN *HAIL MARYS;*
ONE *GLORY BE TO THE FATHER.*

My Own Reflection on
the Fifth Sorrowful Mystery

The
Glorious
Mysteries

THE FIRST GLORIOUS MYSTERY

☐ THE RESURRECTION
When the sabbath was over, Mary Magdalene, Mary, the mother of James, and Salome bought spices so that they might go and anoint him. Very early when the sun had risen, on the first day of the week, they came to the tomb. They were saying to one another, "Who will roll back the stone for us from the entrance to the tomb?" When they looked up, they saw that the stone had been rolled back; it was very large. On entering the tomb they saw a young

man sitting on the right side, clothed in a white robe, and they were utterly amazed. He said to them, "Do not be amazed! You seek Jesus of Nazareth, the crucified. He has been raised; he is not here. Behold the place where they laid him. But go and tell his disciples and Peter, 'He is going before you to Galilee; there you will see him, as he told you.' " Then they went out and fled from the tomb, seized with trembling and bewilderment. They said nothing to anyone, for they were afraid.

When he had risen, early on the first day of the week, he appeared first to Mary Magdalene, out of whom he had driven seven demons. She went and told his companions who were mourning and weeping. When they heard that he was alive and had been seen by her, they did not believe.

Mark 16:1–11

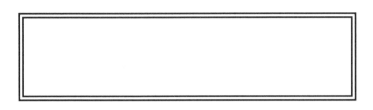

REFLECTION ON THE
FIRST GLORIOUS MYSTERY

The First Glorious Mystery is the Resurrection. We all experience painful moments that make life seem meaningless and hopeless. At such times, we may wonder if life is worth living. But where does the strength and new life come from that helps us to overcome pain and sadness? Does it come from eating the right foods, getting proper exercise and the right amount of sleep? The Resurrection teaches us that it comes from God.

    Early Sunday morning Mary

Magdalene goes to Jesus' tomb. Those who have suffered the loss of a loved one know what she felt in her heart. Only later would she learn that God's love is poured into hearts cracked or broken by the difficulties and sorrows of life. She learned that if we can triumph over death, certainly we can overcome the lesser evils of life with the love God shares with us.

When the women at the tomb realized Jesus had risen from the dead, they must have felt both joy and sorrow—what we often feel when a loved one has died. We are glad their earthly trials are over, but we hate to see them go. We are never without hope, however, when we realize that life is stronger than death.

SAY ONE *OUR FATHER;*
TEN *HAIL MARYS;*
ONE *GLORY BE TO THE FATHER.*

My Own Reflection on the First Glorious Mystery

THE SECOND GLORIOUS MYSTERY

☐ THE ASCENSION
Then he led them [out] as far as
Bethany, raised his hands, and
blessed them. As he blessed them he
parted from them and was taken up
to heaven. They did him homage
and then returned to Jerusalem with
great joy, and they were continually
in the temple praising God.

Luke 24:50–53

REFLECTION ON THE SECOND GLORIOUS MYSTERY

The Second Glorious Mystery is the Ascension. In the Gospel of Luke, the Ascension occurs after Jesus has appeared to his disciples in Jerusalem. He stands in their midst and says, "Peace be with you." They were terrified because they thought they were seeing a ghost. Jesus reassures them, telling them to look at his hands and feet, and to touch him because a ghost does not have flesh and bones. He eats with them, opens their minds to understand his words, and tells them to remain there until they are filled with power from heaven. Finally he leads them to Bethany, blesses them, and is taken up to heaven.

Change can be difficult to accept. "Why," we ask, "does it have to be this way?" The apostles certainly had that question, which can be an invitation to divine wisdom, in their hearts.

The Ascension shows us how much God needs us. Some people ask for more than we have to give. But there are times when the simple things we say or do accomplish more than we could ever imagine.

SAY ONE *OUR FATHER*;
TEN *HAIL MARYS*;
ONE *GLORY BE TO THE FATHER*.

My Own Reflection on the
Second Glorious Mystery

THE THIRD GLORIOUS MYSTERY

☐ THE DESCENT OF THE HOLY SPIRIT

When the time for Pentecost was fulfilled, they were all in one place together. And suddenly there came from the sky a noise like a strong driving wind, and it filled the entire house in which they were. Then there appeared to them tongues as of fire, which parted and came to rest on each one of them. And they were all filled with the holy Spirit and began to speak in different tongues, as the Spirit enabled them to proclaim.

Acts 2:1–4

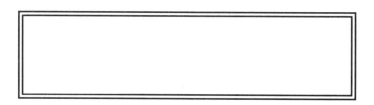

Reflection on the Third Glorious Mystery

The Third Glorious Mystery is the Descent of the Holy Spirit. The Acts of the Apostles tell us the apostles were together in a house that was suddenly filled with the sound of a strong wind. Tongues of fire rested on each of them, and they were filled with the power of the Holy Spirit.

We have felt the presence of the Spirit in moments of insight when all the pieces fall together and we understand something as never before, in moments of love when we discover goodness in others and in ourselves, in moments of unexpected courage and strength that help us to overcome the worst in life. The Spirit, however, cannot work in a heart filled with fear, anxiety, anger, or bitterness. When was the last time you listened to God in your heart? No matter how weak or imperfect we think we are, the Holy Spirit enables us to bring God's love to others.

SAY ONE *OUR FATHER;*
TEN *HAIL MARYS;*
ONE *GLORY BE TO THE FATHER.*

My Own Reflection on
the Third Glorious Mystery

The Fourth Glorious Mystery

☐ The Assumption of the
Blessed Virgin Mary into
Heaven

A great sign appeared in the sky, a
woman clothed with the sun, with
the moon under her feet, and on her
head a crown of twelve stars.

She gave birth to a son, a male
child, destined to rule all the na-
tions with an iron rod. Her child
was caught up to God and his
throne.

Rev 12:1, 5

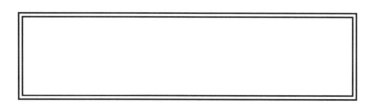

REFLECTION ON THE
FOURTH GLORIOUS MYSTERY

The Fourth Glorious Mystery is the
Assumption. The Church teaches
that the Immaculate Mother of God,
the ever Virgin Mary, having completed the course of her earthly life,
was assumed body and soul to heavenly glory. This belief is not based
on any particular biblical text but on
the faith of the Church. Christian in-
tuition with the guidance of the
Holy Spirit led the Church to believe
that Mary's sharing in her Son's vic-
tory over sin began with her sinless

conception and ended with her Assumption. The Second Vatican Council teaches: "In the bodily and spiritual glory which she possesses in heaven, the Mother of Jesus continues in this present world as the image and first flowering of the Church as it is to be perfected in the world to come."

Reflecting on the special calling of Mary by God and on the closeness of Jesus to his mother, the Church concluded that since it was within Jesus' power to preserve his mother from the corruption of the grave, he certainly granted her this great honor. Is it not fitting that the body that bore the Son of God should be raised up to heaven together with her soul, which was so pleasing to God? If we find this doctrine difficult to believe, it may be because we do not always do all we can for our mothers.

SAY ONE *OUR FATHER;*
TEN *HAIL MARYS;*
ONE *GLORY BE TO THE FATHER.*

My Own Reflection on the Fourth Glorious Mystery

THE FIFTH GLORIOUS MYSTERY

☐ THE CORONATION OF THE
   BLESSED VIRGIN MARY

When the dragon saw that it had been thrown down to the earth, it pursued the woman who had given birth to the male child. But the woman was given the two wings of the great eagle, so that she could fly to her place in the desert, where, far from the serpent, she was taken care of for a year, two years, and a half-year.

Then the dragon became angry with the woman and went off to

wage war against the rest of her off-
spring, those who keep God's com-
mandments and bear witness to
Jesus.

Rev 12:13, 14, 17

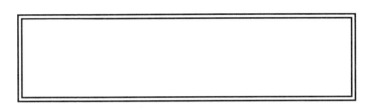

REFLECTION ON THE
FIFTH GLORIOUS MYSTERY

The Fifth Glorious Mystery is the Coronation. Mary is crowned Queen of Heaven and Earth, Queen of Angels and Saints. Imagination does not have any limitations. That is why anticipation and expectation are often greater than what we later experience. Jesus, however, says that the opposite is true about heaven. He tells us that the eye has not seen, the ear has not heard, nor has it entered the heart of man what God has prepared for those who love him. It is a life that will exceed our impossible dreams and our wildest imagination. If this is true, can you imagine what it was like in heaven when Jesus and all the saints and angels greeted Mary after her death? You, too, will be welcomed with joy beyond belief.

Give Mary's love a special place in your heart and invite her to be your heavenly mother.

SAY ONE *OUR FATHER;*
TEN *HAIL MARYS;*
ONE *GLORY BE TO THE FATHER.*

My Own Reflection on
the Fifth Glorious Mystery